Salad Dressings!
Jane Marsh Dieckmann

Edited by Andrea Chesman

The Crossing Press, Freedom, California 95019

Dedication

This book if for Donna, Gay, Inge, Jody, Joyce, and Nancy — who among others have supplied essential recipes and who over the years have plowed through a lot of salads with me — and especially for Pat, who said she needed it.

Cover illustration and design by Betsy Bayley
Medallions in text by Betsy Bayley
Text design by Penknife Studios and Betsy Bayley
Printed in the U.S.A. by McNaughton & Gunn of
Ann Arbor, Michigan

The Crossing Press Specialty Cookbook Series

ISBN 0-89594-223-2 paperback
ISBN 0-89594-224-0 clothbound

Acknowledgments

My thanks to all those good salad makers out there who have provided inspiration, ideas, and support. I am especially grateful to Elaine Gill, who has always believed in me, and to Andrea Chesman, who has gently guided this book to completion.

Contents

Introduction

We are living in a time of great salad eating, and every day more and more salads appear on tables everywhere. Ten or so years ago, a salad bar was a rare and beautiful thing in a restaurant. Today it is a commonplace, and often when discussing good places to eat (especially lunch), we end up talking about the relative virtues of different salad bars. Unquestionably the salad is an increasingly popular part of home menu planning, of restaurant offerings, of our general eating patterns. Is there really a more perfect quick meal? Would any proper dinner not include a salad of some sort? The salad can be the only course you serve at lunch, and it often serves as the main course at dinner.

Salads represent versatile and healthy eating—all those vitamins and minerals, all that filling greenery, all those different nourishing ingredients, all that fiber! They deserve their popularity and their increasingly important role in our lives.

Early definitions of salads consistently refer to a combination of uncooked or cooked foods covered with a savory and piquant dressing and usually served cold. The original salad was a mixture of raw edible leaves of various herbs and plants, eaten with a dressing of *sal* or salt (the origin of the name). Today the name is used for an almost unlimited variety of cooked and uncooked vegetables, fruit, meat, fish, pasta, and grains appearing in some sort of combination.

The important element in this scene is the enhancement of different foods by a dressing. And without any question the dressing is essential. The ingredients of a salad should be of good quality, well prepared, and well presented. What makes or breaks the salad, however, is the dressing. And so salad making means carefully thinking about what foods go well together, what flavors help or inhibit the taste of the dish, and the total meal plan.

In this book you will find many different salad dressings. They are grouped in five chapters, with clear instructions on preparation and storage. My emphasis is on wholesome ingredients, simply and quickly assembled and prepared. And because the main attributes of a salad are that it be tasty, nourishing, and healthful, it is only fitting that the dressing be equally tasty, nourishing, and healthful. Many salad dressings are available commercially, but very few are free of unnecessary and usually unhealthy additives (to emulsify, to beautify, to add or create a certain consistency, to extend the shelf and/or refrigerator life, or to flavor, usually in excess), and many contain abundant and often unneeded calories. So may our salad be a wholesome offering, with a dressing that is light, appropriate, appealing, and not overly fattening. As a special help to the calorie-conscious salad eater (salads are the best answer to the dieter's prayer, in my view), each chapter contains reduced-calorie recipes. Oftentimes the recipes simply are worthy and slender adaptations of the basic and classic dressings.

Almost all dressings keep well when refrigerated, as do the ingredients you need to make them. You can purchase vinegar and oil in quantity, and store it, often without the need for refrigeration. And the same is true for the herbs and spices and other seasonings.

It used to be that we all ate salads on warm summer days as a refreshing escape from hot, heavy meals. Today salads are consumed all year-round; some are served as hot meals and many others at room temperature. There is an enormous variety in salad fare today. More and more unusual salad ingredients are available at the green grocer or in the supermarkets, and people are exploring the possibilities of eating more salads made with legumes, canned and frozen vegetables, not to mention the winter vegetables and different pastas. You can be very creative with your salads. Here is a marvelous opportunity to try out your ingenuity in the kitchen—you can combine different foods, mixtures that would not go together in another form, and achieve a dish with an acceptable and appealing hodgepodge of colors, textures, flavors. Find the right dressing and you have a true culinary achievement.

One chapter contains recipes for salads; do not expect a great number of the standard classics, as a general cookbook will give you recipes. Many of the salads here are unusual combinations or variations on the familiar. Where appropriate, I have provided some suggestions about other dishes to accompany the salad.

Salads are an essential part of my daily diet. My idea of the perfect solution for a brown bag lunch is to make up a salad in a glass or plastic bowl, pour a favorite dressing over and cover it with a tight-fitting lid; I put a slice of bread or cracker with cheese in a plastic bag on top, add a fork and a napkin. The last time I did this, I opened the lid and picked up my fork; the people on each side of me peered into my container—some romaine, a little leftover cooked brown rice and green beans, slices of red pepper, hard-boiled egg, small zucchini, a few alfalfa sprouts, toasted sunflower seeds on top, all with my favorite buttermilk dressing—and both said, "Oh, I wish *I* had thought of that!" Well, now you can. Happy thoughts and happy salad eating!

Buying and Storing Salad Greens

Because freshness is especially important when it comes to salads, you should select your greens carefully. Avoid greens with brown or yellowish edges and spots and always check for bright color, firmness, and crispness. Handle all greens with care. If you buy them loose, shake off as much water as you can. At home, greens are best stored in large plastic bags. Do give them plenty of space. Lettuce taken from your garden can be washed right away. Handle it gently and swish it in a large basin of *cold* water—if you have lots of greens, the kitchen sink will do nicely. Spin or pat the greens dry, and then store. If you leave the lettuce in heads (something like buttercrunch), you will want to wash it again before using it in the salad.

Do not use a knife on your salad greens, but break them with your fingers. Make sure that the greens are chilled and dry before you add the dressing; any water will dilute the flavor. And—very important—unless the recipe says differently, don't add the dressing to the greens until just before serving.

Greens for Salads

An amazing variety is available all year-round these days. So don't settle on iceberg lettuce. It is sweet and crunchy and easy to handle but lacks flavor and gets boring after a while. Remember that the darker the greens, the more vitamins and iron you are likely to get.

Arugula. Also called rugula, raclette, rocket, this is a green you can grow easily from seed (it graciously seeds itself, too). With small, dark green, notched, flat leaves, it has a sharp, peppery flavor and blends well with other greens. It has become very popular in the past few years.

Bibb, Boston Lettuce. These are small heads, pale in color. Bibb lettuce is more crisp and firm than Boston, which is very tender and particularly delicious. Both can be used for garnish or lettuce cups as well as in salads.

Butter or Buttercrunch Lettuce. It is one of the best: crisp and slightly sweet, resembling a small romaine. The leaves are slightly ruffled and dark green on the outside, butter yellow on the inside.

Chicory. Sometimes called curly endive, this feathery, curly green comes in a loose head. It is very firm and crisp, has a bitter tang, and is best combined with other greens.

Dandelion Greens. Here is a great way to clear your lawn! Dig very young dandelions and use the tender, inner leaves. The flavor is quite bitter and invigorating.

Endive. Also called Belgian endive, this unusual green is very popular in Europe. It is a chicory with tight, elongated hearts and leaves ranging in color from very pale green to cream. It is crisp and its flavor is slightly bitter.

Escarole. This has rather large, flat, and coarse leaves, with a slightly bitter taste. Use only the tender green-yellow inner leaves for salads. The outer leaves can be shredded and used in soups.

Iceberg Lettuce. It certainly keeps well and is quite flavorful if you can find it home-grown.

Lamb's Quarters. Along with the dandelion, this weed is abundant and very tasty. The young leaves are mild with a flavor very much like spinach.

Leaf Lettuce. In this category go all the lettuces that don't form a head but have their leaves branching from the stalk. These lettuces come in various colors; the most common are oakleaf, salad bowl, ruby (which has green and red ruffled leaves), and black seeded Simpson.

Romaine. This is an elongated head lettuce, with leaves that go in color from deep green to pale yellow stalks. It has a lovely flavor and is crisp and uncrushable; for this reason it is good in salads that you need to toss a lot.

Spinach. We all know what spinach is and that we were supposed to eat it when we were children. It makes a fine salad green, dark in color and crisp in texture; it also has a delicious, unusual taste. If your children don't buy the Popeye story, sneak the spinach into their salad.

Sprouts. Bean, alfalfa, lentil, and other sprouted seeds make a crunchy and zesty addition to a mixed salad. It is easy and cheap to sprout your own seeds, and this way you can have the quantity you need. You will need to think ahead, however.

Place 1 tablespoon of seeds in a clear glass jar. A pint canning jar with a removable lid and screw band is the best bet for this amount. Fill the jar with warm water, cover it loosely, and let the jar stand out on the counter for 12 hours. Strain off the water (the easiest way to do this is to cover the jar with two layers of cheesecloth, which you secure with the screw band). Then rinse the seeds gently in warm water and drain again. Put the jar in a warm, dark spot (inside a kitchen cupboard is ideal). Once a day, rinse the seeds in fresh warm water and drain. It takes about 4 days for the seeds to sprout, or a little longer in the winter. The sprouts will keep for about a week stored in the refrigerator.

Watercress. Here is a special green, with small, dark leaves. They have a sharp, peppery flavor and are especially good mixed with other greens.

In addition to the leafy salad greens, remember the good vegetables that you can add raw—or barely cooked, if you prefer: green beans, peas, broccoli, cabbage, cauliflower, small zucchini, peppers (green, red, and now yellow), onions in all sizes and colors (especially wonderful is the large, sweet, purplish Bermuda onion, which slices so well and looks so beautiful), mushrooms, kohlrabi, and, of course, carrots, celery, cucumbers, and tomatoes. You can also add cooked corn, artichoke hearts, asparagus, beets, potatoes. And do not forget the grains—brown and white rice, bulgur, kasha, wheat and rye berries.

They add special flavor and texture. Many fresh herbs make delicious additions to salads, and here is a place to follow your own tastes. Particularly popular—minced or chopped—are parsley, oregano, basil, summer savory, not to mention snipped chives and dill weed. Dill heads are really good, too.

A Word on Oil and Vinegar And Other Matters

Oil comes in many different forms. The finest of these is olive oil, which comes in about ten qualities, from pure and extra-virgin oil on down. The fruitiest and most flavorful, in my opinion, comes from Provence, in the south of France; after that come the good Italian and Greek oils. If you use olive oil, get a good quality and store it carefully. I put mine in the refrigerator, which makes it cloudy and somewhat congealed; leaving it at room temperature for a few minutes solves that problem. If the oil is stored at a warm temperature, it becomes rancid. The vegetable oils (corn, soybean, peanut, sunflower, and safflower) are almost without taste, although I personally like sunflower oil for salads. Many people swear by peanut oil, and, if you can get it, walnut oil is simply wonderful. Without entering into the cholesterol controversy, I can point out that olive oil is much higher in unsaturated fatty acids than the others. Remember, too, that oil, any kind, contains about 120 calories per tablespoon, so dressings with little or no oil are desirable for dieters.

The best vinegar is wine, either white or red. Vinegars come in many qualities too, and it is best to buy a good one. If you like herbed vinegars, you can make your own by adding the herb of your choice—tarragon seems to be preferred—to the vinegar for about two weeks. Fruit vinegars, especially raspberry, have become popular recently. If you can get some, try balsamic vinegar. It is Italian, from Modena (like Luciano Pavarotti), and is a full-bodied dark vinegar that has been aged for years in wooden casks. Its flavor is bright, less acidic than usual vinegars, and rich.

It is wise and tastier to grind your pepper fresh each time, and please use fresh lemon and lime juice. Mustards are really a question of taste, but for recipes in this book, use a good French Dijon-style mustard. The coarse grained country-style mustards are also delicious.

Equipment

You really don't need anything special. I like to serve salad in a glass bowl, because it looks so pretty. Just make sure that the bowl is large enough to allow you to turn the ingredients over carefully, without crowding or dumping them over the edge. If you have a good paring knife and some sort of jar to shake up your dressings, you are in business.

To my mind, the best salad-making aid is the spinner. This gadget really does get the water off washed greens quickly, effortlessly.

I use a garlic press often; my favorite vinaigrette dressing takes freshly pressed garlic. An herb mincer comes in handy, as do a lemon reamer and a pepper mill. A wire whisk is especially useful. On the more expensive side, it is infinitely easier to make many dressings, especially mayonnaise, if you have a blender or food processor.

A Note on Seasoning

My particular taste calls for less pungent flavoring and a smaller quantity of salad dressing than usual. Also I don't like salt very much. If you find these recipes need more of something, just feel free to add to your own taste. That is what cooking is all about anyway.

1
Mayonnaise

This is the most popular of the oil sauces. The name is French, coming from the expression, *à la mayonnaise*, a usage that dates from 1807; the term is thought to be a corruption of *à la mahonnaise*, named in remembrance of the seizure of Port-Mahon on the island of Minorca (the French took it from the British in 1756). Whatever its source, mayonnaise is a very widely used dressing in world cuisine and commonly used as a base for many sauces and salad dressings. It is firm and golden and traditionally is made with egg yolks and a high quality oil, usually olive oil, with some seasonings — salt and pepper and vinegar — added. Mayonnaises today often contain some quantity of mustard, and many are made with whole eggs.

Despite popular belief, mayonnaise is easily made. *And* homemade mayonnaise is vastly superior to any commercial product. Because it contains no preservatives, however, you should keep it refrigerated and use it up in five days. The important thing to keep in mind is to have all ingredients at room temperature before you start to make the mayonnaise. Although much more easily made in a blender or food processor, mayonnaise can be done by hand. Use the recipe for Mayonnaise I (page 19); place the egg yolks in a large bowl and slowly — I do mean slowly, drop by drop — add the oil, while you stir or whisk constantly. After the mixture begins to thicken, you can add the oil in a thin stream, until you have the desired consistency. Add the remaining ingredients. If the mayonnaise gets too thick, stir in a little more lemon juice. If, by chance, your mixture doesn't coagulate, start with a new egg yolk in a different bowl, and slowly beat the first mixture into it.

You can add all sorts of lovely things to mayonnaise — herbs, horseradish, sweet or sour pickles, garlic, tomato paste.

Uses for mayonnaise are many and varied. Any salad that isn't principally loose greens can be dressed with mayonnaise.

Mayonnaise I

2 egg yolks
¼ teaspoon salt
2 teaspoons Dijon-style mustard
1 tablespoon lemon juice
1 cup olive oil

Yield: About 1½ cups

This recipe, as well as the one following, is most easily made in a food processor or blender.

Fit the metal blade in a food processor. Add all the ingredients, except the oil, and process for about 10 seconds, or until combined. Slowly add the oil in a steady stream through the feed tube. The mixture will begin to thicken in less than a minute. If you use a blender, put a third of the oil in the container with the other ingredients, cover, and process for a few seconds. Then, with the blender still on at low speed, slowly pour in the remaining oil.

Keep the mayonnaise refrigerated in a covered container and plan to use it all within 5 days.

Mayonnaise II

1 cup oil, preferably sunflower or
   safflower
2 eggs
2 tablespoons lemon juice or white wine
   vinegar
1 teaspoon sugar
1 teaspoon dry mustard
½ teaspoon salt
Dash cayenne

Yield: About 1⅔ cups

Unlike the previous recipe, this mayonnaise uses whole eggs and has more ingredients and a stronger flavor.

Pour ¼ cup of the oil into a food processor (using the steel or plastic blade) or blender. Add the other ingredients. Process for 5 to 10 seconds or blend at high speed. While the motor is running, add the remaining ¾ cup oil in a fine stream. When the mayonnaise is thick and smooth, turn off the machine. Store, covered, in the refrigerator.

Variation

Slimmer Mayonnaise (Reduced-calorie recipe). Omit the sugar and reduce the salt to ¼ teaspoon. Blend equal parts of mayonnaise with plain yogurt. Season, if desired, with some celery seeds and minced chives.

Aïoli

4 large garlic cloves
1 teaspoon Dijon-style mustard
½ teaspoon salt
¼ teaspoon white or lemon pepper
1 egg
¾ cup olive oil
Lemon juice

Yield: About 1 cup

This strong sauce, a staple in most French kitchens, originates in Provence and is especially common in Marseille, where everyone eats a dish of the same name—mixed seafood or snails smothered in the sauce.

Fit the metal blade in a food processor. With the machine on, drop the garlic through the feed tube and chop. Scrape down the sides of the bowl and add all the ingredients, except the oil and lemon juice. Process for about 10 seconds. Slowly add the oil through the feed tube and process until the mixture thickens, about 30 seconds. Add lemon juice to taste. Store in the refrigerator.

Use in fish soups, as a spread on cold meats, or as dressing for any fish and/or vegetable salad.

Creamy Mustard Dressing

1 small egg yolk
1 tablespoon hearty Dijon-style or
 Dusseldorf mustard
Dash Tabasco sauce
½ teaspoon minced garlic
1 teaspoon red or white wine or balsamic
 vinegar
½ cup olive oil
2 teaspoons fresh lemon juice
1 teaspoon heavy cream
Salt and pepper

Yield: About ¾ cup

This dressing has more mustard flavor than standard mayonnaise. It is particularly good over thinly sliced ham or slightly cooked and chilled whole green beans or broccoli florets. It too can be made in a blender or food processor; just follow the procedure for making the mayonnaises.

Place the egg yolk in a mixing bowl and beat well. Add the mustard, Tabasco, and garlic. Stir in the vinegar. Beat vigorously with a wire whisk to blend the ingredients, and while beating, slowly add the oil. Keep beating until the dressing is thickened and well blended. Add the lemon juice and beat in the heavy cream. Add salt and pepper to taste. Cover and store in the refrigerator.

Soy-Sherry Mayonnaise

2 tablespoons dry sherry
1 egg yolk
1½ tablespoons lemon juice
1 tablespoon Dijon-style mustard
1 tablespoon dark soy sauce
1 teaspoon sugar
½ teaspoon minced fresh ginger or
   ¼ teaspoon ground
¼ cup olive oil
¼ cup safflower or peanut oil

Yield: About ¾ cup

This Oriental combination goes well with a salad of chicken strips, snow peas, water chestnuts, and scallions, with lots of toasted sesame seeds over the top.

Mix all the ingredients, except the oils, in a food processor or beat together in a small bowl. Blend well. Gradually add the oils, processing or beating constantly until the mixture is emulsified. Chill well before serving.

Green Goddess Dressing

4 anchovy fillets, finely cut, or
   2 tablespoons anchovy paste
3 tablespoons finely chopped scallions,
   including some tops
1 tablespoon chopped fresh parsley
1 teaspoon minced fresh tarragon or
   ¼ teaspoon dried
1 tablespoon tarragon wine vinegar
Pinch salt and pepper
1½ cups Mayonnaise I or II
   (pages 19, 20)

Yield: About 1¾ cups

Here is a beautiful dressing, pale green with green flecks. Traditionally it is served over a mixture of romaine, escarole, and chicory. You can omit the anchovies; some recipes do. If you can get Italian parsley, do use it here. With a food processor, the metal blade will finely chop the anchovies, scallions, parsley, chives, and tarragon before you blend in the mayonnaise.

Mix the ingredients gently until blended. Chill thoroughly before serving.

Herbed Mayonnaise

1½ cups Mayonnaise II (page 20)
2 tablespoons finely chopped fresh
   parsley
2 tablespoons finely cut chives
2 tablespoons chopped fresh dill or
   tarragon

Yield: About 1¾ cups

This is another green dressing, less strong in flavor than the preceding, and one where you can use any herbs to your taste. Do not try to combine too many at a time.

Combine the ingredients and chill for several hours before serving.

Variations

Italian Mayonnaise. Prepare Mayonnaise II and add ¼ teaspoon lemon pepper. While blending, add ½ cup chopped fresh Italian parsley and coarsely chopped fresh basil leaves combined.

Spinach Mayonnaise. Measure ½ cup very dry raw spinach leaves (no stems, please) and puree in a blender or food processor. Combine with the other ingredients.

Rémoulade Sauce

2 cups Mayonnaise I or II
  (pages 19, 20)
1 large hard-boiled egg, finely chopped
2 tablespoons finely chopped capers
1 tablespoon finely chopped fresh parsley
  or a combination of parsley and chives
1 teaspoon lemon juice
Salt and pepper

Yield: About 2¼ cups

The French, who invented this one too, serve this sauce on grated raw vegetables, celery root in particular. The Creole version is excellent with seafood salads or as a dip for shrimp and raw vegetables.

Blend all the ingredients together, adding the salt and pepper to taste. You can omit the salt and add ½ teaspoon anchovy paste instead. Refrigerate for several hours before using to blend the flavors.

Variation

Creole Mayonnaise. Add to the above ¼ cup sour cream, ¼ cup catsup, ¼ cup minced shallots or scallions, 4 teaspoons coarse-grained mustard, 2 tablespoons tarragon vinegar, 2 tablespoons chopped dill pickle, and 2 teaspoons paprika.

Egg and Curry Mayonnaise

2 eggs
1 cup Mayonnaise I (page 19)
½ cup shredded Emmenthaler or
   Swiss-type cheese
2 tablespoons white wine vinegar
2 tablespoons red wine or
   balsamic vinegar
2 tablespoons minced fresh parsley
1 garlic clove, minced
½ teaspoon curry powder
½ teaspoon beef bouillon powder
Half-and-half

Yield: About 1½ cups

This hearty dressing goes well over any mixed greens or a chef's salad with turkey and ham. Or try it as a variation over the usual tuna or potato salad. Add more curry if you like it that way.

Combine all the ingredients, except the half-and-half, in a blender or food processor. Whirl at high speed for about 10 seconds, or until thoroughly blended. Thin to a desired consistency with the half-and-half. Store in the refrigerator in a covered container.

Soy-Curry Mayonnaise

1 cup Mayonnaise II (page 20)
1 tablespoon lemon juice
1 teaspoon (or more) curry powder
1 teaspoon soy sauce
¼ teaspoon salt
¼ teaspoon pepper

Yield: About 1 cup

This brightly colored dressing is delicious over chicken and fruit combinations—Indian Melon Salad (page 116), for example—or tuna or cooked vegetable salads, such as mixed legumes and water chestnuts.

Blend everything together in the order given. Chill for several hours before using. Store any extra in a covered container in the refrigerator.

Variation

Thin Soy-Curry Mayonnaise (Reduced-calorie recipe). Substitute Mock Mayonnaise (page 62) for about one-half of the mayonnaise in the recipe.

Bleu Cheese Dressing

1 garlic clove, minced
3 tablespoons chopped chives
1 tablespoon lemon juice
½ cup sour cream
1 cup Mayonnaise I (page 19)
½ cup crumbled bleu cheese
   (about 2 ounces)
Salt and freshly ground pepper

Yield: 2¼ cups

This rich, very flavorful dressing is popularly served over firm greens, such as hearts of lettuce or romaine.

Combine the garlic, chives, and lemon juice in a bowl. Add the sour cream, mayonnaise, and cheese. Blend everything well and then season to taste with salt and pepper. Cover and refrigerate for several hours before using.

Variation

Roquefort Dressing. Substitute Roquefort cheese for the bleu cheese.

Cabbage Slaw Dressing

2 tablespoons oil
1 tablespoon lemon or lime juice
½ teaspoon Dijon-style mustard
Dash paprika
¼ teaspoon celery salt
¼ teaspoon celery seeds
¼ cup Mayonnaise II (page 20)
Salt and pepper

Yield: About ½ cup

Many people make their coleslaw with a vinaigrette or sweet and sour dressing. This dressing is creamier and somewhat milder; it contrasts well with the crunch of the cabbage in the slaw.

Blend all the ingredients, except the mayonnaise and salt and pepper. Stir in the mayonnaise and season to taste with salt and pepper. Chill for several hours before using.

Hearty Sauce

½ cup Mayonnaise II (page 20)
¼ cup sour cream
¼ cup strong beef broth
2 tablespoons red wine or
   balsamic vinegar
Salt and pepper

Yield: About 1 cup

Pour this dressing over a combination of cooked vegetables—such as fresh cut corn, green beans, carrot pennies, peas—mixed with green pepper strips, chopped red onion, and tomato wedges.

Beat together the mayonnaise and sour cream in a bowl. Blend in the broth and vinegar and season to taste with salt and pepper. Keep chilled until you are ready to serve.

Variation

Skinny Hearty Sauce (Reduced-calorie recipe). Use Mock Mayonnaise (page 62) for part or all of the Mayonnaise II and substitute plain yogurt for the sour cream.

2
Vinaigrettes

The vinaigrette is the classic dressing in France, a thin, piquant sauce made by combining oil and vinegar with seasonings. The word itself is a diminutive of the French term for vinegar and dates from the 14th century. So here is a truly traditional salad dressing with a long history.

Over the years the classic vinaigrette has changed and knows many variations. It is one of the easiest recipes possible, as you combine the ingredients in a bowl or cup and mix them with a fork, or you measure everything in a jar, cover with a tight-fitting lid, and shake well. In its pure form, vinaigrette is made with two or more parts oil to one part vinegar and has only salt and pepper for seasoning. Very often today a vinaigrette has mustard added. The amounts of oil and vinegar can vary (James Beard, for example, recommends 4 parts oil to 1 part vinegar). The dressing can indeed change taste noticeably with different vinegars and oils (due to considerable variation in strength and flavor). For the best vinaigrette, select a strong flavored olive oil and a good quality wine vinegar. Many recipes use part or all lemon juice for the vinegar, which—strictly speaking—makes them no longer vinaigrettes. But even so, such a change does not really alter the basic qualities—a tart, tangy flavor and a thin consistency—of the real thing.

As I am always looking for ways to cut calories, and remember that a tablespoon of oil contains about 120 of them, I often make vinaigrette with as much vinegar as oil (and sometimes even more; here, by the way, is an excellent place to try balsamic vinegar). Sharp zesty tastes appeal to a lot of us. To this mixture I add no salt, no pepper, but a dollop of coarse-grained mustard and a pressed clove of garlic. This makes a wonderful topping for crisply cooked green beans and broccoli, with some chopped scallions and a few slices of sweet red pepper. If you don't mind your eyes watering from time to time, try it. You can also substitute plain yogurt for a part of the oil; this addition counteracts the sharpness of the vinegar and makes a creamy topping.

Because of its thinness and almost infinite adaptability, the vinaigrette is the best dressing for salads of mixed greens. It is also marvelous for grain salads and over cooked vegetables, as well as meats and fish. Although potato and tuna salads are traditionally made with mayonnaise, a vinaigrette dressing is delicious and provides a pleasant change.

Basic Vinaigrette

2 tablespoons red or white wine or
    balsamic vinegar
4 tablespoons olive oil
½ teaspoon salt
¼ teaspoon pepper

Yield: About ⅓ cup

The purists among cooks say that it is best not to make more vinaigrette dressing than you need for one salad. Thus the basic recipe is for a small quantity. My experience is that it keeps well if you keep it refrigerated, covered tightly.

Combine the ingredients in a glass jar, cover with a tight-fitting lid, and shake well. Or mix with a fork in a bowl. Store any extra in the refrigerator.

Variations

Hearty Vinaigrette. Omit the salt and add 2 tablespoons minced onion, ½ teaspoon instant chicken broth powder, ¼ teaspoon Worcestershire sauce, and 1 garlic clove, pressed.

Herbed Vinaigrette. Add 2 tablespoons minced fresh basil, 1 tablespoon minced fresh parsley, and 1 large garlic clove, minced. This is especially good for tomatoes. Or try the combination of 1 tablespoon minced fresh parsley and 1 teaspoon minced fresh dill weed, which is good on seafood and cucumber salads. Or add a combination of ½ teaspoon crumbled leaf marjoram, 2 tablespoons chopped fresh parsley, and 2 tablespoons chopped scallions for chicken and pasta salads.

Processor Herbed Vinaigrette. Put the ingredients in a food processor along with 2 garlic cloves, 2 teaspoons Dijon-style mustard, some basil leaves, and sprigs of parsley. Process until well blended. The result will be a creamy dressing.

Roquefort Vinaigrette. Add ¼ teaspoon mild paprika and 3 ounces (about 4 tablespoons) crumbled Roquefort cheese to the dressing. Adjust the seasonings.

Spicy Vinaigrette

½ cup oil
3 tablespoons lemon juice
2 tablespoons white wine vinegar
1 teaspoon sugar
1 teaspoon coriander seeds
1 teaspoon cumin seeds
1 garlic clove
Dash cayenne

Yield: About ¾ cup

Try this exotic and very lively dressing on mixed greens, vegetables, or meat salads. Make it ahead so that the flavors have a chance to develop.

Combine all the ingredients in a food processor or blender. Blend for about 30 seconds or until well combined. Store in the refrigerator for several days before using.

Sweet-Sour Vinaigrette

2 to 3 tablespoons sugar
1 teaspoon dry mustard
½ teaspoon salt
½ teaspoon celery seeds
1½ teaspoons minced onion
¼ cup white wine vinegar
½ cup oil

Yield: About 1 cup

This dressing makes a fine accompaniment to some of your more unusual combinations. Try it over torn fresh spinach, shredded purple cabbage and/or carrots, some slivered almonds, and raisins.

Combine all the ingredients in a jar. Cover tightly and shake well. Chill the dressing thoroughly and then shake again. This keeps well in the refrigerator.

Garlic Vinaigrette

2 garlic cloves
1 egg
2 cups oil
1 tablespoon dried fines herbes
  (1 teaspoon each parsley and chervil,
  ½ teaspoon each tarragon and chives,
  or use a commercial mixture)
2 teaspoons Dijon-style mustard
Salt and pepper
Juice of two lemons
Lemon rind

Yield: About 2 cups

This recipe was given to me many years ago by a fascinating Italian woman, who distinguished herself in my mind by whirling her salad greens in a little basket around and around her head. I had never seen anything like it before. Try this dressing over a crisp salad of escarole, chicory, and firm iceberg lettuce.

Crush the garlic with some salt. Beat the egg into the oil and then stir in the garlic, fines herbes, mustard, and salt and pepper to taste. Beat this mixture well. Then add the lemon juice and grate some lemon rind into the mixture. Beat well again. This keeps well when stored covered in the refrigerator. Mix it up thoroughly before serving.

Variation

Three Bean Vinaigrette. Substitute ⅔ cup white wine vinegar for the lemon juice, omit the lemon rind, and increase the garlic to three cloves. Serve over chilled mixed cooked beans or navy beans cooked with crumbled thyme.

Parmesan Dressing

1 egg
¼ cup lemon juice
¼ cup olive oil
1 garlic clove, pressed
1 teaspoon Worcestershire sauce
¼ cup grated Parmesan cheese
Salt and pepper
1 tablespoon Dijon-style mustard
   (optional)

Yield: About ¾ cup

This goes well on a spinach, bacon, and sliced mushroom salad. If you pour it over romaine pieces, add some anchovies and croutons, you have a Caesar Salad.

In a jar that can be fitted with a tight lid, beat the raw egg with a fork; add the lemon juice and beat again. Then add the other ingredients, adding salt and pepper to taste, and shake to mix thoroughly. If you like, add 1 tablespoon Dijon-style mustard. Store in the refrigerator.

Lemon Garlic Dressing

¼ cup olive oil
¼ cup lemon juice
¼ teaspoon salt
1 heaping teaspoon pressed garlic
1 tablespoon minced fresh parsley
(optional)

Yield: ½ cup

Mix this simple dressing for Tabouli (page 112) or other grain salads. The combination of garlic and lemon juice is perfect.

Blend the oil with the freshly squeezed lemon juice. Add the salt and garlic. The parsley adds color and consistency.

Variation

Lemon Sherry Dressing. Add 2 teaspoons grated lemon rind and 2 teaspoons dry sherry to the dressing.

Lemon Mustard Dressing

¼ cup lemon juice
2 teaspoons Dijon-style mustard
2 teaspoons sugar
¼ cup minced scallions
6 tablespoons olive or vegetable oil
½ teaspoon salt
Dash pepper
2 tablespoons chopped fresh dill weed or
 1 tablespoon dried

Yield: About 1 cup

Try this over lightly cooked carrot pennies, sliced beets, or young whole green beans. It also makes an elegant simple salad poured over romaine and topped with toasted sliced almonds.

Combine all the ingredients in a jar, cover and shake until well blended. Chill for at least 2 hours before using. Store covered in the refrigerator.

Honeyed Vinaigrette

½ cup cider vinegar
½ cup safflower or peanut oil
5 tablespoons honey
1 tablespoon water
1 teaspoon salt

Yield: About 1½ cups

This sweet-sour dressing is best over sliced red cabbage. Chill the salad for several hours before serving.

Combine all the ingredients in a small saucepan over medium heat. Bring to a boil. To make a salad, pour over sliced cabbage, blend well, and taste to adjust the seasoning. Any extra dressing will keep for several weeks in the refrigerator, and can be used cold over mixed green salads.

Variation

Poppy Seed Vinaigrette. Add 1 teaspoon dry mustard and 1 tablespoon poppy seeds.

Curried Vinaigrette

¼ cup oil
1 tablespoon curry powder
⅓ cup white wine vinegar
2 tablespoons lemon juice
2 tablespoons honey
1 cup raisins (optional)

Yield: About ¾ cup (without the raisins)

This dressing has a wonderful bite and is delicious on grain and legume salads.

Heat the oil in a small saucepan, stir in the curry powder, and cook for a minute or so. Then add the remaining ingredients and simmer for about 6 minutes. While it is still warm, pour over vegetables and/or grains.

Soy-Sesame Dressing

¼ cup olive oil

2 tablespoons tarragon vinegar

2 tablespoons soy sauce

¼ teaspoon minced fresh tarragon leaves or a pinch dried

¼ teaspoon dry mustard

¼ teaspoon oriental sesame oil or ½ teaspoon tahini (sesame paste)

Freshly ground pepper

Yield: About ½ cup

This light oriental dressing goes well over bibb lettuce by itself or with some watercress, sliced cucumber, and mandarin oranges added.

Mix all the ingredients in a small bowl, adding the pepper to taste. Store in the refrigerator.

Variations

Sesame Seed Dressing. Reduce the soy sauce to 2 teaspoons and add 1 tablespoon sugar and 1 tablespoon sesame seeds.

Zesty Dressing. Omit the tarragon and sesame oil. Add 1 tablespoon sugar, 2 teaspoons lemon juice, and 2 generous dashes Tabasco sauce.

Ginger Dressing

½ cup white wine vinegar
¼ cup soy sauce
1 teaspoon sugar
1 teaspoon dry mustard
½ teaspoon (or more) ground ginger
1 garlic clove, minced

Yield: About ¾ cup
Reduced-calorie recipe

Because this dressing has plenty of flavor and no oil at all, it makes a fine choice for the dieter. It is very thin and dark colored. Try it as a marinade for cooked chicken chunks, sliced almonds, and scallions, which you serve over shredded lettuce or Chinese cabbage and garnish with radishes.

Combine the ingredients in a bowl or glass jar and whisk them until well blended. Store in the refrigerator.

Pasta Salad Dressing

½ cup safflower or sunflower oil
¼ cup white wine vinegar
3 tablespoons lemon or lime juice
2 large garlic cloves, pressed
½ teaspoon honey
1 tablespoon plain yogurt
1 teaspoon Dijon-style mustard
½ teaspoon salt
Pepper

Yield: About 1 cup

Although this was designed for pasta combinations, it is the most popular all-purpose dressing in my house. It is creamy in appearance and keeps very well.

Put everything in a jar, cover, and shake well. You can cut the garlic in half, leave it in the dressing for several hours, and then remove it. To my mind, however, one of this dressing's strong points is the special taste that only fresh garlic can give. Store tightly covered in the refrigerator.

Bacon Vinegar Dressing

4 bacon slices
2 teaspoons sugar
2 tablespoons cider vinegar
2 tablespoons water
¼ teaspoon pepper
Dash salt

Yield: About ½ cup

This hot dressing is poured over leaf lettuce to make wilted salad. Without the sugar it goes over German Potato Salad (page 119). It also is especially good on slightly cooked green beans with celery, legume combinations, or torn spinach with sliced mushrooms and chopped cooked chicken livers.

Fry the bacon until crisp, remove from the pan, drain on paper towels, and crumble. Pour all but 2 tablespoons bacon fat from the pan and stir in the remaining ingredients. Heat to boiling. Keep warm and pour over the salad just before serving.

Cooked Vinaigrette

1 tablespoon cornstarch
1 cup water
2 tablespoons lemon juice
2 tablespoons white wine vinegar
2 tablespoons oil
1 teaspoon sugar
1 teaspoon horseradish
1 teaspoon Dijon-style mustard
2 tablespoons chopped sweet or
    dill pickles
1 teaspoon Worcestershire sauce
¼ teaspoon salt
¼ teaspoon paprika
1 tablespoon minced fresh parsley

Yield: About 1½ cups
Reduced-calorie recipe

To this easy low-calorie recipe you can add various extra ingredients according to your particular taste. It is very good over slightly cooked green vegetables.

Mix the cornstarch and water together in a saucepan and cook over low heat, stirring, for about 5 minutes. When the mixture is clear, remove from the heat, and cool. Then blend in the remaining ingredients with a beater or use a food processor or blender. Store covered in the refrigerator.

Variation

Celery Seed Vinaigrette (Reduced-calorie recipe). Omit the horseradish and pickles, increase the mustard to 2 teaspoons. Stir in 1 teaspoon celery seeds.

3
Dairy-Based Dressings

These dressings have a dairy base—buttermilk, cottage cheese, yogurt, cream. As to be expected, they are creamy in appearance, and often quite thick in consistency. And because the base can be very low in calories—especially buttermilk and plain yogurt—these dressings are a wonderful aid to the dieter. Additional benefits are their high protein and calcium content. And of all the salad dressings, they are probably the easiest to make. Most of them will keep up to a week, but make sure they are always kept refrigerated.

Dieckmann House Dressing

2 cups buttermilk
1 tablespoon minced fresh parsley
2 teaspoons grated lemon rind
2 teaspoons celery seeds
1 teaspoon minced fresh summer savory
1 teaspoon minced fresh marjoram
1 teaspoon minced fresh basil
1 teaspoon cut chives
½ teaspoon finely cut fresh dill weed
½ teaspoon garlic powder or 2 small
  garlic cloves, pressed
Salt and pepper

Yield: About 2¼ cups
Reduced-calorie recipe

This is a more complicated version of the Basic Buttermilk Dressing. The ingredients can be changed and quantities varied to your particular taste. The amounts given are for fresh herbs; use about one-third the amount if you use dried herbs.

Put all the ingredients in a large jar or bottle, adding salt and pepper to taste. Cover with a tight-fitting lid. Shake well. Let the dressing stand at room temperature for an hour or so and then chill. It will keep for at least a week stored in the refrigerator.

Basic Buttermilk Dressing

1 cup buttermilk
1 garlic clove, pressed
¼ teaspoon sugar
1 teaspoon Dijon-style mustard
¼ teaspoon salt (seasoned salt, if you like)
⅛ teaspoon pepper

Yield: About 1 cup
Reduced-calorie recipe

This dressing can be varied in any number of ways. It is a basic ranch-type dressing, delicious over mixed greens and sliced tomatoes.

Combine all the ingredients in a jar and cover with a tight-fitting lid. Shake well to blend. Let the dressing stand a few minutes before serving. Store in the refrigerator.

Variations

Dill Buttermilk Dressing (Reduced-calorie recipe). Stir in 1 teaspoon minced fresh dill weed or ½ teaspoon dried. This is very good over sliced tomatoes.

Lemon Creamy Dressing (Reduced-calorie recipe). Instead of the Dijon-style mustard, use ¼ teaspoon dry mustard. Add 1 tablespoon sour cream, 1½ teaspoons lemon juice, and ½ teaspoon paprika. Shake well before serving. This is very good over fish salads.

Zingy Buttermilk Dressing (Reduced-calorie recipe). Add ½ cup chili sauce, 1 tablespoon prepared horseradish, 1 tablespoon grated onion, a few drops Tabasco sauce, 1 teaspoon Worcestershire sauce, and 1 teaspoon sugar. This will add zip to any mixed green or fish salad. The additions increase the yield to 1½ cups.

Creamy Yogurt Dressing

1 cup plain yogurt
2 tablespoons buttermilk
½ teaspoon grated lemon rind
1 tablespoon Worcestershire sauce
1 tablespoon onion juice
Salt

Yield: About 1¼ cups
Reduced-calorie recipe

Here is a dressing that lends itself to infinite variations. Add some horseradish or curry powder for meat or seafood salads, or some Parmesan or Roquefort cheese for green salads, or poppy seeds for fruit or vegetable salads. And if you want a really high-protein version, stir in ½ cup dry milk powder.

Combine all the ingredients, adding salt to taste, and blend well. Store covered in the refrigerator. The calorie count is about 7 per tablespoon.

Variation

Dilled Yogurt Dressing (Reduced-calorie recipe). Omit the lemon rind and Worcestershire sauce. Stir in ½ teaspoon dill seeds or 1 teaspoon minced fresh dill weed (or ½ teaspoon dried), ¼ teaspoon dry mustard, ¼ teaspoon minced garlic, and freshly ground pepper to taste.

Hundred Island Dressing

1 cup plain yogurt
¼ cup catsup or chili sauce
1 garlic clove, minced
2 tablespoons finely chopped pickle
2 tablespoons finely chopped green
   pepper
2 tablespoons chopped celery
1 hard-boiled egg, chopped
2 tablespoons chopped scallions or chives
1 teaspoon Dijon-style mustard
1 teaspoon paprika
Salt
1 tablespoon Worcestershire sauce
   (optional)
1 tablespoon chopped green olives
   (optional)

Yield: 1¾ cups
Reduced-calorie recipe

Here is the reduced-calorie version of Thousand Island Dressing, and one that is much higher in protein. It is very good over a cold fish salad or sliced tomatoes.

Blend the yogurt, catsup or chili sauce, garlic, pickle, green pepper, celery, egg, scallions or chives, mustard, and paprika in the order given. Add salt to taste and adjust the seasoning. If you like, add the Worcestershire sauce and green olives. Chill thoroughly and store in the refrigerator.

Lemon Yogurt Dressing

1 cup yogurt
¼ cup lemon juice
½ cup dry milk powder
2 tablespoons honey
½ teaspoon salt
¼ teaspoon curry powder
1 teaspoon minced fresh basil or
  ½ teaspoon crushed dry
3 tablespoons chopped chives
3 tablespoons minced fresh parsley

Yield: About 2¼ cups
Reduced-calorie recipe

Extremely simple and quick to make, this protein-rich dressing is smooth, with a creamy color. It is especially good over cooked bean combinations. Thinned with a little buttermilk it goes well over the milder salad greens.

Whisk the yogurt until smooth. Stir the lemon juice and milk powder together to make a smooth paste; then whisk this into the yogurt. Blend in the honey, then the remaining ingredients. This keeps well in the refrigerator.

Variation

Seeded Yogurt Dressing (Reduced-calorie recipe). Omit the herbs and add 1 teaspoon poppy seeds or 1 teaspoon sesame seeds to the dressing.

Mock Mayonnaise

1 cup plain yogurt
1 egg yolk, raw
1 egg yolk, hard-boiled and sieved
Salt and pepper
1 teaspoon Dijon-style mustard
1 teaspoon lemon juice
2 scallions, minced
Honey
Instant vegetable broth powder (optional)
Dried herbs (optional)

Yield: About 1 cup
Reduced-calorie recipe

I make this dressing more often than any other, especially in the summer. It makes a delicious, low-calorie substitute for mayonnaise in most recipes and also serves as a tasty sauce over chilled cooked green vegetables and potatoes.

Put the yogurt in a bowl and whisk in the raw egg yolk. Stir in the remaining ingredients, adding honey to taste—you will need very little, about ¼ teaspoon—and blend thoroughly.

I often omit the cooked egg yolk even though it does add substance and color to the dressing. Also, I often add more mustard. If you want more flavor, stir in some instant vegetable broth and/or dried herbs of your choosing (½ teaspoon dried dill weed is very good).

Near East Dressing

1 tablespoon lemon juice
1 tablespoon olive oil
2 teaspoons chopped fresh mint or
  ½ teaspoon dried
1 tablespoon minced fresh dill weed or
  ½ teaspoon dried
¾ teaspoon salt (seasoned if you like)
1 cup plain yogurt

Yield: About 1 cup
Reduced-calorie recipe

The combination of mint and dill with the creamy yogurt gives this authentic dressing a special quality. It is particularly good over a salad of torn lettuce, sliced cucumbers, and green grapes.

Combine all the ingredients, except the yogurt, and mix well. Then stir them into the yogurt. Chill for several hours so that the flavors can blend. Store in the refrigerator.

Cottage Cheese Dressing

2 cups small-curd cottage cheese
¼ cup finely chopped onion
¼ to ½ teaspoon salt
2 tablespoons red or white wine or
    balsamic vinegar
2 teaspoons Dijon-style mustard
1 teaspoon celery seeds

Yield: About 2¼ cups
Reduced-calorie recipe

This is my favorite dressing for potato salad.

Stir the ingredients together in a bowl and mix well. Taste to adjust the seasoning. Chill for several hours before using. Store in the refrigerator.

If you prefer a smoother, creamier dressing, substitute 1 cup milk or buttermilk for 1 cup of the cottage cheese and whirl everything in the blender or food processor until smooth.

Variation

Herbed Cottage Cheese Dressing (Reduced-calorie recipe). Add 1 tablespoon minced fresh parsley and 1 teaspoon minced fresh dill weed or fresh rosemary leaves.

Light Green Goddess Dressing

1 cup low-fat cottage cheese
¼ cup skim milk
1 teaspoon anchovy paste
1 tablespoon lemon juice
1 hard-boiled egg
1 teaspoon celery salt
1 teaspoon dry mustard
1 large bunch fresh parsley, chopped
   (4 cups)
¼ cup chopped chives

Yield: About 2 cups
Reduced-calorie recipe

Here is another low-calorie version of a classic rich dressing.

If you have a food processor, use it to chop the parsley and chives before you measure them. Then combine all the ingredients and blend until smooth. Keep the dressing refrigerated in a covered container.

Sour Cream Dressing

¾ **cup sour cream**
1 **teaspoon Dijon-style mustard**
1 **teaspoon lemon juice**
½ **teaspoon honey or 1 teaspoon sugar**
½ **teaspoon salt**
Dash pepper

Yield: About ¾ cup

Here is a light and fresh dressing, excellent over a mixture of cooked chicken, diced celery, and seeded grapes.

Mix the ingredients together and chill for several hours to allow the flavors to blend. This keeps well in the refrigerator.

Variation

Sesame Cream Dressing. Omit the mustard and increase the lemon juice to 1 tablespoon. Add 1 tablespoon toasted sesame seeds. This combination is good over sliced cucumbers and onions.

Onion Cream Dressing

½ sweet red onion, thinly sliced
2 tablespoons red wine vinegar
¼ cup sugar
¼ cup heavy cream
2 hard-boiled eggs, chopped
2 slices bacon, cooked, drained, and
  crumbled

Yield: About ¾ cup

This colorful, chunky dressing makes the perfect accompaniment to the classic spinach salad, to which you can add mandarin orange sections and chopped walnuts for a change.

Combine the ingredients in a jar and marinate overnight in the refrigerator before serving.

Creamy Cooked Dressing

1 teaspoon Dijon-style mustard
½ teaspoon salt
1 tablespoon flour
½ teaspoon celery seeds
½ cup skim milk
1 garlic clove (optional)
1 egg yolk, beaten
3 tablespoons white wine vinegar
½ teaspoon sugar
½ teaspoon instant vegetable broth
  powder

Yield: About ¾ cup
Reduced-calorie recipe

Despite its resemblance to mayonnaise, this dressing has only about 12 calories per tablespoon. It is very smooth with an appealing pale yellow color.

Mix together the mustard, salt, flour, and celery seeds in a small saucepan. Place on the stove over low heat and slowly add the milk (which you may like to warm in advance), stirring constantly. Cook, stirring, until the sauce has thickened and is smooth. Add the garlic clove, cook slowly for about 5 minutes, and then remove it.

Whisk in the egg yolk and cook for 3 minutes more, stirring all the time. Remove from the heat and stir in the vinegar, sugar, and vegetable broth until well blended. Chill before using and store extra in the refrigerator.

4
Vegetable-Based Dressings

This series of dressings depend on vegetables (or a fruit, as in the case of the avocado) for their main ingredient. They are colorful and rich in flavor. Many of them are also low in calories. If you make your own tomato juice, then you will know all the ingredients of your dressing. Try to use vegetables that are as fresh as you can get them. Most of these dressings are most easily made in a blender or food processor. The more you blend or process, the smoother the dressings will be. When you serve salads with these dressings, do keep in mind their distinct colors, which can beautifully enhance the general appearance of your meal.

Fresh Tomato Herb Dressing I

2 pounds ripe tomatoes, peeled, seeded, and diced
¾ teaspoon salt
1 teaspoon sugar (or more to taste)
¼ teaspoon pepper
3 tablespoons red wine or balsamic vinegar
¼ cup olive oil (French, if you can get it)
2 tablespoons minced fresh chives
2 tablespoons minced fresh parsley

Yield: About 3 cups

Here is a truly delicious and fresh tasting tomato sauce for cooked vegetables. Try it over barely cooked (or raw) zucchini slices garnished with golden brown toasted pine nuts (pignoli) and you will have a summer salad fit for the gods.

In a blender or food processor, whirl about half the diced tomatoes with the salt, sugar, pepper, and vinegar. When the mixture is smooth, and with the machine on, slowly add the olive oil. Combine the tomato puree with the remaining tomato cubes and stir in the chives and parsley. Taste and adjust the seasonings. Serve at once. Any remainder can be stored in the refrigerator.

Fresh Tomato Herb Dressing II

¾ cup peeled, seeded, and diced
   tomatoes
1 garlic clove
½ teaspoon salt
¼ teaspoon pepper
½ teaspoon Dijon-style mustard
2 tablespoons lemon juice
2 fresh basil leaves or 2 fresh tarragon or
   parsley sprigs

Yield: About 1 cup
Reduced-calorie recipe

This tart fresh dressing contains 3 calories per tablespoon.

Combine all the ingredients in a blender or food processor and blend until very smooth, about 30 seconds. Cover and store in the refrigerator.

French Tomato Dressing

¼ cup tomato sauce
⅓ cup red wine vinegar
1 cup oil
1 tablespoon sugar
1 teaspoon salt
¼ teaspoon pepper
1 tablespoon chopped fresh basil leaves
   or 1 teaspoon dried
1 teaspoon Worcestershire sauce
½ teaspoon Dijon-style mustard
Dash hot pepper sauce
1 garlic clove

Yield: About 1⅔ cups

Make this dressing in a food processor or blender, and the results will be very smooth. It has a lovely red color and goes very well over vegetable salads, mixed greens, even citrus fruits or apples. Use homemade tomato sauce if you possibly can.

Combine all the ingredients in a food processor or blender and whirl until smooth and the garlic is minced. Chill in a cruet or covered container until you are ready to use it. This dressing will keep for at least a week in the refrigerator.

Thick French Dressing

⅔ cup catsup
1 cup oil (peanut or corn oil preferred)
½ cup sugar
1 medium-size onion, cut up
1 garlic clove, halved
2 teaspoons paprika
½ cup red wine vinegar
1 teaspoon salt
Juice of 1 lemon

Yield: About 2½ cups

This is a rich, smooth, colorful, and flavorful dressing. It goes well over mixed greens, especially dark ones. If you like a sweeter dressing, add more sugar.

Combine the ingredients in a blender or food processor in the order given. Blend until very smooth. Store in the refrigerator.

Easy Bacon Dressing

½ **pound bacon**
¼ **cup catsup**
¼ **cup tarragon vinegar**
¼ **cup olive oil**

Yield: About 1 cup

Designed to go over torn spinach leaves, this lively and colorful dressing also makes a fine accompaniment to torn lettuce or a combination of crisp, slightly bitter greens.

Fry the bacon until crisp. Drain and crumble. Combine the other ingredients and mix well. Stir in the bacon. Pour over the spinach or greens and serve immediately. Store any extra dressing in the refrigerator.

Mock Louis Dressing

¼ cup tomato juice
1 cup low-fat cottage cheese
1 hard-boiled egg
1 teaspoon Dijon-style mustard
2 tablespoons finely chopped onion
2 tablespoons minced fresh parsley

Yield: About 1½ cups
Reduced-calorie recipe

Here is a low-calorie, protein-rich alternative to the traditional Sauce Louis. It is pale pink and perfect with tuna, shrimp, crabmeat, or lobster.

Combine the tomato juice, cottage cheese, egg, and mustard in a blender or food processor. Whirl until very smooth. Stir in the onion and parsley. Chill thoroughly before serving, and store any extra dressing in the refrigerator.

Tomato Juice Dressing

½ cup tomato juice
2 tablespoons lemon juice
1 tablespoon minced onion
¼ teaspoon celery salt
½ teaspoon dried parsley
1 garlic clove, pressed
Horseradish

Yield: About ¾ cup
Reduced-calorie recipe

Thin in consistency and zesty in taste, this dressing carries the possibilities of many variations. Use homemade tomato juice, if possible.

Combine the ingredients in a jar, adding horseradish to taste. Cover with a tight-fitting lid and shake very well. This keeps well in the refrigerator.

Variation

Tomato Juice and Soy Dressing (Reduced-calorie recipe). Omit the salt, parsley, garlic, and horseradish. Stir in 1 tablespoon soy sauce and ¼ teaspoon dried basil.

Tomato Soup Dressing

1 can (10 ounces) tomato soup
¾ cup sugar
1 teaspoon pepper
½ cup oil
½ cup red wine vinegar
1 teaspoon Worcestershire sauce
Salt (optional)

Yield: About 2½ cups

Canned soups are an ingredient that I usually avoid, but this dressing is quite special. It makes a beautiful topping over cooked vegetables, especially beets and carrots.

Stir the ingredients together. Taste and add salt if desired. Chill for several hours before serving. This dressing will keep for at least 10 days in the refrigerator.

Vegetable Juice Dressing

1 can (12 ounces) mixed vegetable juices
2 tablespoons tarragon vinegar
1 teaspoon Dijon-style mustard
1 teaspoon Worcestershire sauce
½ teaspoon sugar
Dash paprika

Yield: About 1¾ cups
Reduced-calorie recipe

This is among my oldest recipes, and still a favorite over mixed greens. It is zesty and low in calories. You can add herbs to your taste and also stir in some grated Parmesan cheese.

Combine all the ingredients in a jar. Cover with a tight-fitting lid. Shake vigorously. This keeps for at least 10 days stored in the refrigerator.

Variation

Vegetable Juice and Yogurt Dressing (Reduced-calorie recipe). This is a milder and creamier version. Make the dressing as above and stir in ½ cup plain yogurt and some grated Parmesan cheese to taste.

Avocado Dressing

1 ripe avocado, peeled and chopped
1 ripe tomato, peeled, seeded, and
   chopped
4 teaspoons lime or lemon juice
½ onion, cut in pieces
3 tablespoons oil

Yield: About 1 cup

This dressing is smooth and beautiful in color. One should eat it all up, however, as the avocado will discolor.

Blend all the ingredients in a blender or food processor until smooth. Serve the dressing immediately.

Variation

Creamy Avocado Dressing. Omit the tomato and stir in ½ cup yogurt or sour cream, ½ teaspoon ground cumin, and ¼ teaspoon cayenne pepper.

Guacamole

1 large or 2 medium-size avocados
3 tablespoons minced scallions
2 tablespoons minced green pepper
1 tablespoon lime juice
¼ teaspoon salt
¼ teaspoon chili powder
Dash Tabasco sauce
Dash pepper
1 garlic clove, bruised
Mayonnaise II (page 20)

Yield: About 1 cup

Because of the mayonnaise covering that prevents discoloration, this guacamole can be made ahead of time. Serve this beautiful green sauce over torn salad greens garnished with tomato wedges.

Make sure the avocado is dead ripe. Peel and mash it in a medium-size bowl. Then mix in the scallions and green pepper along with the lime juice, salt, chili powder, Tabasco, and pepper. Use the garlic to rub the inside of a small bowl and then discard it. Put the mixture into the prepared bowl and cover with enough mayonnaise to prevent the air from reaching the avocado mixture. Chill thoroughly until serving time. Just before serving, stir the mayonnaise into the mixture. Do use it all in one sitting.

Cucumber Dressing

1 medium-size to large cucumber
2 cups plain yogurt
1 cup sour cream
2 tablespoons minced fresh dill weed or
   1 tablespoon dried
Salt and pepper
3 garlic cloves
Small quantity olive oil

Yield: About 3 cups

Peel the cucumber and cut in pieces. Blend in a food processor with the yogurt, sour cream, and dill. Add salt and pepper to taste and adjust the seasoning. Cut the garlic and mash the cloves in the oil (just enough to make a paste). Quickly combine this with the other ingredients. Chill thoroughly, preferably overnight, to blend the flavors. This keeps in the refrigerator for several days.

Variations

Raita (Reduced-calorie recipe). Omit the sour cream, dill, garlic, and oil. Blend in 1 small onion and 1 teaspoon ground cumin. This is traditionally served as an accompaniment to shish kebab.

Eggplant Sauce

1 medium-size eggplant
¼ cup minced onion
2 medium-size tomatoes, peeled and
  chopped
1 garlic clove, minced
2 tablespoons chopped fresh parsley
2 tablespoons oil
2 tablespoons red wine or
  balsamic vinegar
½ teaspoon dried marjoram
½ teaspoon salt
Pepper

Yield: About 2½ cups
Reduced-calorie recipe

Serve this wonderful Greek mixture over crisp lettuce and garnish with parsley.

Place the whole eggplant in a shallow pan, prick the skin in several places, and bake for about 1 hour at 350° F. Dip in cold water and peel off the skin. Dice the eggplant and measure out 2 cups.

Combine the eggplant with the other ingredients in a food processor and blend until smooth. Taste and adjust the seasonings. This dressing is good served at room temperature. Store extra in the refrigerator.

Tofu-Tahini Dressing

½ **pound tofu**
¼ **cup tahini (sesame paste)**
1 tablespoon sesame or sunflower oil
1 tablespoon soy sauce
2 large garlic cloves, cut in pieces
½ **teaspoon grated fresh ginger**
3 tablespoons lemon juice
Honey
Water

Yield: About 2 cups

Creamy and smooth, this high-protein dressing goes well on crisp greens or mixed grain salads.

Combine the tofu, tahini, oil, soy sauce, garlic, ginger, and lemon juice in a blender or food processor. Add a little honey and blend until smooth. Taste and add more soy sauce if desired. Thin to a desired consistency with water. Store the dressing in the refrigerator.

Variation

Herbed Tofu Dressing. Omit the honey and add ¼ teaspoon dried dill weed, or 1 teaspoon of your favorite fresh herbs, minced. You can also stir in ¼ cup grated Parmesan cheese.

5
Sweet Dressings

These dressings are used almost exclusively for fruit salads. Generally they are thicker than other dressings and often they are seasoned with spices. If you are interested in sweetening with honey, here is a place to experiment; several recipes that follow will offer suggestions.

In European cuisine, a fruit salad is almost invariably a dessert—which often goes by the name of *macédoine* (in French) or *macedonia* (Italian)—consisting of various fruits, cut up and mixed together. Much as I admire the Europeans and their cooking, they have missed out on something, as salads made of fruit alone or of fruit combined with meats and crisp vegetables and greens are delicious and play an important role in our meals. When trying to work fruit into the menu, do keep in mind the many fruit salads.

Celery Seed Dressing

⅓ cup sugar
1 teaspoon dry mustard
½ teaspoon salt
2 tablespoons grated onion
⅓ cup white wine vinegar
1 tablespoon lemon juice
1 cup safflower, sunflower, or peanut oil
1 tablespoon celery seeds

Yield: About 1½ cups

This is a thick, pale-colored dressing, a classic of its kind. Use white wine vinegar to keep it light in appearance.

Combine the sugar, mustard, and salt in a small bowl. Stir in the onion, vinegar, and lemon juice. Slowly pour in the oil, mixing well with a wire whisk. Add the celery seeds. You can serve this dressing immediately. Store any extra in the refrigerator.

Variation

Honey Celery Seed Dressing. Omit the sugar and reduce the onion to 1 teaspoon. Combine 1 teaspoon paprika with the mustard and salt and blend ⅓ cup honey with the vinegar before you stir it in with the onion and lemon juice.

Poppy Seed Mustard Dressing

1 small white onion
1 cup olive oil
⅓ cup white or red wine vinegar
½ cup sugar
1 teaspoon salt
1 teaspoon dry mustard
2 tablespoons poppy seeds

Yield: About 1½ cups

Easily made in a blender or food processor, this dressing goes especially well over citrus salads.

Cut the onion into small pieces and mince in a blender or food processor. Add the remaining ingredients, except the poppy seeds and blend until well combined. Transfer to a bowl or glass jar and stir in the poppy seeds. Cover and refrigerate before serving.

Fruit Juice French Dressing

¼ cup unsweetened pineapple juice
¼ cup orange juice
1 tablespoon lemon juice
3 tablespoons white wine vinegar
⅛ teaspoon ground cloves or nutmeg
1 teaspoon honey or 1½ teaspoons sugar
Pinch salt

Yield: ¾ cup
Reduced-calorie recipe

At about 3 calories per tablespoon, this nicely colored, tart, and thin sauce makes a refreshing topping for chilled mixed fruit and citrus salads.

Combine all the ingredients in a jar. Cover with a tight-fitting lid. Shake well. Chill before serving. Keep this dressing refrigerated and shake well before using.

Variation

Minted Fruit Juice Dressing (Reduced-calorie recipe). Add 1 teaspoon minced fresh mint leaves or ½ teaspoon dried, and let the dressing stand at room temperature for several hours before chilling.

Dieckmann Special Dressing

¼ to ⅓ cup sugar
1 tablespoon flour
½ teaspoon salt
½ teaspoon dry mustard
1 egg
½ cup white vinegar
¼ cup water
1 cup plain yogurt
1 tablespoon (or more) poppy seeds

Yield: About 2 cups
Reduced-calorie recipe

I always keep a jar of this dressing on hand in the refrigerator. The basic boiled dressing (without the yogurt and poppy seeds) will keep for about a month. A favorite luncheon or dinner salad for me is a combination of sliced or cut fresh fruits—pears, peaches, apples, bananas, plums, red or green grapes—with some homemade cranberry sauce, covered with this dressing. For crunch I sprinkle granola on top.

Mix the sugar (use ⅓ cup if you like a sweeter dressing), flour, salt, and mustard in a small saucepan. Add the egg and whisk it in, making a smooth paste. Combine the vinegar and water and slowly stir it in. Cook over medium heat until the mixture is boiling, stirring constantly. If you have a wire whisk, here is the time to use it. Boil the dressing for 2 minutes, still stirring. Strain it into a jar and cool. To make the complete recipe, stir in the yogurt and poppy seeds.

To make a smaller amount, mix roughly equal amounts of dressing and yogurt and put in the quantity of poppy seeds you prefer. In either case, store the dressing in the refrigerator.

Yogurt and Fruit Juice Dressing

1 cup plain yogurt
1 tablespoon honey
2 tablespoons orange juice concentrate
2 tablespoons unsweetened pineapple
   juice
Pinch cinnamon
Pinch salt
2 tablespoons chopped raisins
1 tablespoon chopped walnuts or pecans
1 tablespoon flaked coconut

Yield: About 1½ cups
Reduced-calorie recipe

This is a creamy and crunchy dressing with a lovely fruit flavor.

Mix everything together in a bowl. Taste and adjust the seasonings. If the dressing is too thick, add a little buttermilk or more fruit juice. Store in the refrigerator.

Creamy Orange Dressing

1 package (8 ounces) cream cheese,
   softened
Dash salt
1 teaspoon dry mustard
2 teaspoons grated orange rind
½ cup orange juice
1 tablespoon honey

Yield: About 1 cup

This tangy sweet dressing goes best with a combination of fruits or fruits and greens. If you want to serve a citrus fruit combination, this is ideal. Try to make it with fresh orange juice.

Combine the ingredients in a blender or food processor fitted with a steel blade, and whirl at high speed until smooth. Serve at once. Store any extra in the refrigerator.

Variation

Cottage Cheese and Orange Dressing (Reduced-calorie recipe). Substitute 1 cup cottage cheese, 8 ounces farmer cheese, or a combination of the two for the cream cheese. You can also use part (but no more than one-half) tofu.

Honey Cream Dressing I

1 cup Mayonnaise I (page 19)
½ teaspoon salt
1 tablespoon lemon juice
2 tablespoons honey
¼ teaspoon ground nutmeg
1 cup whipped cream

Yield: About 2 cups

This is rich and luscious and elegantly accompanies any fancy molded fruit or chicken salad. There will be no discussion of calories here.

Stir together all the ingredients, except the whipped cream, and blend well. Gently fold in the whipped cream and serve immediately. This dressing will keep in the refrigerator but will become thinner as the whipped cream breaks down.

Honey Cream Dressing II

1 cup (8 ounces) creamed cottage cheese
¼ cup chopped pecans
¼ cup light cream
1 tablespoon honey
¼ teaspoon ground allspice

Yield: About 1½ cups

This dressing is also creamy and luscious and lower in calories than the preceding one. If you'd like to try it with even fewer calories, use low-fat cottage cheese and substitute milk or plain yogurt for the cream.

Fit the steel blade in the food processor and add all the ingredients. Blend until smooth. For a more textured dressing, simply press the cottage cheese through a sieve into a small bowl and stir in the remaining ingredients. In either case, cover and chill well. Stir the dressing just before serving. Be sure to keep the remainder refrigerated.

Cranberry Dressing

⅔ **cup raw cranberries**
2 **tablespoons apple cider**
3 **tablespoons honey**
1 **tablespoon lemon juice**
⅓ **cup plain yogurt**
2 **tablespoons oil**
Salt (optional)

Yield: About 1 cup

This is particularly good at Thanksgiving time, when the cranberries are plentiful in the market. It is fairly thick, and a lovely pink color with red flecks from the cranberries. It is especially good over a combination of crisp apple chunks, grated carrots, and raisins.

Grind the cranberries in a meat grinder or chop them fine in a food processor. Put them in a bowl and stir in the cider, honey, lemon juice, yogurt, and oil in the order given. Taste the dressing and add some salt, if you want it. Store in the refrigerator.

6
The Salads

These recipes represent some, though by no means all, of my favorite salads. The dressings for the particular salads are recommended, but do feel free to vary the repertory.

One way to reduce calories in salads made with mayonnaise is to substitute Mock Mayonnaise (page 62) for the equal amount of dressing in the following recipes. Be sure you have included the additional seasonings where appropriate. As Mock Mayonnaise is thinner in consistency, you may prefer to mix in some regular mayonnaise, which works very well too.

Super Tossed Salad

4 cups torn romaine, raw spinach, leaf
  lettuce, endive
½ cup arugula
3 icicle radishes, cut in strips
½ cup cooked brown rice or bulgur
1 cup cooked vegetables (sliced beets, cut
  green beans, broccoli florets, diced
  potatoes, asparagus in 1-inch pieces)
2 ripe tomatoes, in wedges, or 1 cup
  cherry tomatoes
¼ cup toasted sunflower seeds
¼ cup crumbled feta cheese or
  2 tablespoons grated Parmesan cheese
Basic Buttermilk Dressing (page 56) or
  Dieckmann House Dressing (page 55)
Crunchy Topping (page 135)

Yield: 4 to 6 servings

This is my favorite mixed salad. The ingredients can be varied to suit your particular taste. The salad disposes of leftover cooked vegetables in the refrigerator.

In a large salad bowl, combine the salad ingredients in the order given. Pour the dressing over and toss gently.

Sprinkle the topping over the salad. Serve at once.

Tomato and Mozzarella Salad

4 large ripe tomatoes, peeled and sliced
  ¼ inch thick
1 pound mozzarella, thinly sliced
Herbed Vinaigrette (page 37)
Freshly ground pepper
1 Spanish onion, peeled, thinly sliced,
  and separated into rings
Flat anchovy fillets (optional)
Fresh parsley
Black olives

Yield: 4 to 6 servings

This salad should be enjoyed when the tomatoes are fresh and ripe. It is a delicious side dish for steaks or fish on the grill, along with rice or potatoes. You can arrange the salad in individual servings but it is really most striking on a large platter.

Alternate the tomato and mozzarella slices, overlapping, on a large platter. Drizzle the dressing over the salad. Sprinkle with fresh pepper and arrange onion rings and anchovies on top. Garnish with parsley and olives. Chill well before serving.

Spinach Bacon Salad

1 pound fresh spinach
Easy Bacon Dressing (page 75)
2 scallions, minced
¼ cup sunflower seeds
¼ pound fresh mushrooms, sliced
2 hard-boiled eggs, in wedges
Cherry tomatoes or tomato wedges

Yield: 6 servings as a main course

This traditional salad is served with a bright, unconventional dressing. Enjoy it for lunch or for dinner.

Wash and dry the spinach and tear it into bite-size pieces. Put in the refrigerator, rolled in a tea towel, to keep crisp. Prepare the dressing.

When you are ready to serve the salad, arrange the spinach, scallions, and sunflower seeds in a large bowl. Place the sliced mushrooms over the top and pour the dressing over. Garnish with the egg wedges and tomatoes. Serve at once.

Many Bean Salad

1 cup cooked garbanzo beans, drained
1 cup cooked kidney beans, drained
1 cup cooked black beans, drained
1 cup cooked cut green beans
2 cups Lemon Yogurt Dressing (page 61)
1 cup chopped celery
½ cup chopped green or red pepper
½ cup chopped scallions

Yield: 8 to 10 servings

Here is a creamy variation on the classic Three Bean Salad. Serve it very cold.

If you are cooking your own beans, boil them separately. This way they keep their individual colors. Cook them until tender but still firm. Drain well.

Prepare the dressing, doubling the recipe. Combine the cooked beans with the other ingredients and pour the dressing over. Chill the salad for several hours before serving.

Variation

Three Bean Salad. Omit the green beans and use 1 cup of the dressing.

Bean and Egg Salad

3 cups cooked green beans
2 hard-boiled eggs, chopped
½ to 1 cup Mayonnaise II (page 20)
Milk or buttermilk (optional)
Salt and pepper

Yield: 3 to 4 servings

This salad was standard summer fare when I was growing up, and even now we always eat it whenever my brother shows up. My mother strongly feels that this salad should have a sweet boiled dressing. If your taste resembles hers, try Dieckmann Special Dressing (page 90) or Poppy Seed-Mustard Dressing (page 88) instead of the mayonnaise I use. And the best of luck to you.

Combine the beans and eggs in a large salad bowl. Pour the dressing over — you may want to thin it first with a little milk or buttermilk. Add salt and pepper to taste. Serve chilled or at room temperature over a bed of lettuce and garnish with tomato wedges.

Green Pepper Boats

3 large green peppers
1 onion, grated
½ cup grated cabbage
2 tomatoes, chopped
2 small zucchini, diced
1 scallion, chopped
5 radishes, diced
½ red pepper, finely chopped
1½ tablespoons chopped fresh parsley
½ cup finely chopped broccoli
Cucumber Dressing (page 82)
Spinach leaves or leaf lettuce

Yield: 6 servings

Here is a crunchy study in color, especially green, which includes the dressing. The pepper boats make a good side dish to go with beef cooked on a grill or with omelettes and other egg dishes. And they use everything in the garden.

Cut the peppers in half lengthwise, remove the seeds and membrane, wash, and drain.

Combine the onion, cabbage, tomatoes, scallion, radishes, red pepper, parsley, and broccoli in a bowl. Stir in enough dressing to bind them together.

Stuff the pepper halves with the vegetable mixture and arrange on a plate covered with spinach leaves or leaf lettuce. Chill before serving.

Sunshine Salad

2½ **pounds carrots**
1 **cup chopped onion**
1 **cup chopped green pepper**
Tomato Soup Dressing (page 78)

Yield: 10 servings

Here is another colorful salad, sometimes called "golden pennies" salad. As it is made ahead of time and keeps very well, it is ideal for a picnic.

Scrape the carrots and cook whole in salted water for about 20 minutes. Drain, cool, and thinly slice crosswise. You should have 5 to 6 cups.

Mix together the onion, green pepper, and dressing and pour over the carrots. Cover and refrigerate for at least 12 hours before serving.

Western Health Salad

1 large head romaine
¼ pound Monterey Jack cheese
2 large oranges, peeled, sectioned, cut in small pieces
½ cup raisins, either dark or golden
¼ cup sunflower seeds
1 cup Creamy Orange Dressing (page 93)

Yield: 6 servings
(4 as a main dish)

I have yet to meet anyone who does not like this salad enormously. It has all the qualities of a perfect salad: color, an unusual and tangy dressing, and a variety of tastes and textures. It makes a fine main dish for a luncheon (hot corn bread or cornmeal rolls make a good accompaniment) and goes well at dinner with chicken, turkey, or ham. It is quickly and easily made.

Break up the romaine in bite-sized pieces into a large salad bowl. Shred the cheese on top and then add the oranges, raisins, and sunflower seeds. You can vary the amounts according to what you have available and your taste; I make this salad very often and don't measure anything! Pour the dressing over and toss gently until well mixed. Serve at once.

Worth Street Waldorf Salad

3 large crisp apples
¾ cup chopped celery
½ cup chopped dry-roasted peanuts
½ cup raisins
Dieckmann Special Dressing (page 90)
Lettuce

Yield: 6 servings

This is my variation on the traditional salad. Use crisp, red-skinned apples and don't peel them. I have often made this salad with Granny Smiths, which are quite green. The salad looks different, but is just as good. Serve this with chicken or ham dishes.

Use a glass salad bowl if you have one. Cut the apples in pieces and add the celery, peanuts, and raisins. Pour enough dressing over to moisten the salad. You can eat this right away or chill it until you are ready for it. Serve it on a bed of lettuce.

Avocado and Grapefruit Salad

2 large grapefruit
1 large or 2 small avocados
Celery Seed Dressing (page 87)
Lettuce

Yield: 6 servings
(3 as a main dish)

This is a rich and beautiful salad, combining the smooth creamy blandness of the avocado with the tart juiciness of the citrus fruit. It makes a wonderful accompaniment to any roast chicken, turkey, or ham. Or try it with warm batter buns or oatmeal rolls to create an elegant luncheon.

Peel and cut the grapefruit in sections, draining the juice. Peel the avocado and cut it in sections. Prepare the dressing. Arrange the grapefruit and avocado sections on beds of lettuce and drizzle the dressing over. Serve at once.

Southern Fruit Ambrosia

Fruits (unpeeled apples, bananas, grapes, pineapple, peaches, pears, plums, blueberries, orange sections, cantaloupe, honeydew melon)
Honey Cream Dressing I (page 94)
Shredded coconut
Fresh mint

Back in the good old days, this salad was usually made with canned fruit cocktail and served with tiny marshmallows in it. Times have changed, but the idea of the luscious fruit mixture with a creamy dressing lives on. This salad goes particularly well with baked ham.

Slice the fruit as desired and combine it in a large glass bowl. Spoon the dressing over and sprinkle the coconut over the top. Chill thoroughly before serving. Garnish with fresh mint.

Curried Rice Salad

½ cup uncooked whole wheat berries
1½ cups uncooked brown rice
2 cups cooked soybeans
1½ teaspoons salt
1⅓ cups shredded cheddar cheese
2 onions, chopped
6 celery stalks with tops, chopped
Curried Vinaigrette (page 46)
Salad greens

Yield: About 24 servings
(12 as a main dish)

This recipe makes a vast quantity and is the best contribution to a dish-to-pass picnic that I know of. It also serves as a wonderful conversation piece, as people are unable to identify the wheat berries. Some ingredients require extra time, so plan ahead.

Don't substitute anything for the wheat berries, unless you want to use rye berries instead. Cook the first three ingredients separately and be sure to allow enough time.

Cover the wheat berries with boiling water and cook until tender, about 1 hour. When they are done, drain them. Then add ½ teaspoon of the salt and ⅔ cup of the cheese. Stir until the cheese melts and then chill.

Bring 3½ cups water to a boil in a large saucepan and slowly pour in the brown rice. Reduce the heat, cover, and cook for

45 to 50 minutes. Stir in the remaining 1 teaspoon salt and ⅔ cup cheese and chill.

Drain and chill the soybeans. You can do all of this the day before, if you want.

Chop the vegetables and set aside. Prepare the dressing. While the dressing simmers, toss the grains to separate the kernels.

At this point—in the words of one friend—"take a washtub." Use the largest receptacle you can find; a huge porcelain jam kettle is ideal. Combine the grains, soybeans, and chopped vegetables. Pour the dressing over and toss again. Chill thoroughly. Serve on a bed of fresh greens.

Tabouli

1 cup bulgur (toasted cracked wheat)
1½ cups boiling water
½ teaspoon salt
Lemon Garlic Dressing (page 43)
1 cup tightly packed chopped fresh
   parsley
½ cup chopped scallions
½ cup cooked garbanzo beans
2 large tomatoes, cut up
1 tablespoon chopped fresh mint leaves
   (optional)

Yield: 6 to 8 servings

This salad takes some time, but it is well worth it. It is the garlic lover's delight and a very special addition to any buffet or picnic. Tabouli can be served on a bed of lettuce or as stuffing for pita bread, green peppers, or tomatoes.

Put the bulgur in a large bowl and pour the boiling water over the top. Add the salt and stir well. Allow this to stand for 20 minutes while you make the dressing.

Pour the dressing (use the whole recipe) over the bulgur and blend it in.

Prepare the parsley, scallions, and garbanzos and put them on top. Refrigerate the salad for several hours. Just before serving, add the tomatoes and the traditional mint. Stir everything together.

Salade Provençale

1 can (6½ ounces) tuna, drained and
flaked
1 medium-size green pepper, cut in strips
1 cup crisply cooked green beans, cut in
1-inch pieces
1 small tomato, cut in wedges
½ cup diced boiled potatoes
¼ cup chopped scallions
2 hard-boiled eggs, chopped
Garlic Vinaigrette (page 40)
Lettuce

Yield: 4 servings as a main dish

Here is a variation of the traditional French dish called Salade Niçoise. It is less heavy and strong in flavor. It is generally served as a main dish; all you need are some rolls or crusty bread, butter, and a good firm cheese for accompaniment.

Combine the salad ingredients in a large bowl and pour enough dressing over to moisten everything. Stir well and allow to marinate for several hours. You can serve this particular salad at room temperature on a bed of crisp lettuce.

Dilly Tuna Salad

1 can (20 ounces) pineapple chunks
1 can (6½ ounces) tuna, drained and
    flaked
1 cup sliced cucumber
¼ cup toasted sunflower seeds
Crisp salad greens
½ teaspoon salt
½ teaspoon fresh dill weed or
    ¼ teaspoon dried (if you are using
    Mock Mayonnaise)
⅓ cup Mock Mayonnaise (page 62) or
    Dilled Yogurt Dressing (page 58)
Fresh dill
Green or red grapes

Yield: 4 servings as a main dish

With its combination of tuna and fruit, this salad makes a refreshing and nourishing luncheon dish. Serve it with crusty French bread and a rather salty cheese, such as Gouda or Jarlsberg.

Drain the pineapple and reserve 2 tablespoons of the juice.

Toss the pineapple, tuna, cucumber slices, and sunflower seeds. Line a bowl with the greens and pour the salad in.

Blend the reserved juice, salt, and dill with the mayonnaise or dressing and pour over the salad. Garnish with sprigs of dill and green or red grapes if desired.

Spinach-Noodle and Tuna Salad

4 cups cooked spinach noodles
1 can (6½ ounces) tuna, drained and
flaked
1 cup chopped celery
1 large carrot, coarsely grated
1 small to medium-size zucchini, coarsely
grated
¾ cup chopped scallions
1 cup alfalfa sprouts
1 teaspoon dried oregano
Salt and pepper
Pasta Salad Dressing (page 49)

Yield: 4 to 6 servings as a main course

Make sure the noodles are well drained and cooled. Mix them with the tuna, vegetables, oregano, and salt and pepper to taste. Toss lightly with the dressing. Taste and adjust the seasoning. Chill for several hours before serving. Any leftovers will keep well in the refrigerator for several days.

Variation

Chicken Pasta Salad. Substitute 2 to 2½ cups cubed cooked chicken for the tuna and dried dill weed for the oregano. Add ½ cup sliced radishes and ½ cup shredded Swiss cheese. You can substitute cooked, drained macaroni for the noodles, if you prefer.

Indian Melon Salad

2 cups cubed cooked chicken or turkey
1 can (5 ounces) water chestnuts, drained
   and sliced
1 cup seedless green or red grapes
¾ cup chopped celery
1 cup Soy-Curry Mayonnaise (page 28)
1 cup honeydew melon balls or cubes
1 cup cantaloupe balls or cubes
Boston lettuce

Yield: 6 servings

This chicken and fruit main dish is among my most popular salads. When the melons are in season, it is the perfect choice for a luncheon or special supper. I like to serve it with crisply cooked young green beans and hot whole wheat or cornmeal rolls.

Combine the chicken, water chestnuts, grapes (cut them in half if they are large), and celery. Pour the dressing over the mixture and mix well. Then add the melon balls and toss lightly. Chill thoroughly. Arrange the lettuce to form cups on individual salad plates or a platter. Spoon the salad into the lettuce cups and serve at once.

Italian Chicken Salad

1 cup diced cooked chicken
¾ cup cubed boiled potato
¼ cup cooked quartered artichoke hearts
1 cup chopped celery
½ cup thinly sliced raw young zucchini
½ cup alfalfa sprouts
1 cup Tomato Juice Dressing (page 77)
Torn lettuce

Yield: 2 servings

This main dish salad is designed for dieters. It is also pretty and unusually tasty. Serve it with broccoli, asparagus, or very young green beans, lightly steamed and dressed with lemon juice. Add a little rye krisp or melba toast and you're thin already!

Combine the chicken and vegetables in a bowl. Heat the dressing to the boiling point, then simmer for 5 minutes. Pour the hot dressing over the salad. Cover and chill. Serve on torn lettuce.

Tropical Chicken Salad

1 pound cooked breast of chicken or
turkey, cut in ½-inch cubes
(about 2 cups)
4 celery stalks, sliced
1 can (16 ounces) pineapple chunks,
drained
½ cup chopped salted peanuts
½ cup raisins
4 scallions, chopped
Curried Vinaigrette (page 46) or Honeyed
Vinaigrette (page 45) with ½ teaspoon
curry powder added

Yield: 4 servings

This salad can be made with either chicken or turkey, and you can add other fruits to it. It serves as a main dinner course, with a rice and vegetable combination or with a vegetable combination such as fresh green peas and cut corn, or sautéed zucchini and onions.

Combine the salad ingredients. Pour enough dressing over to moisten the salad and toss. Chill for several hours before serving.

German Potato Salad

4 potatoes
1 medium-size onion
Bacon Vinegar Dressing (page 50)

Yield: 2 servings as a main dish

One of the easiest hot salads, this is also one of the most popular. Serve it with a mixed green salad, covered with a bland, creamy dressing, or with a crisply cooked green vegetable such as asparagus, broccoli, or green beans.

Boil the potatoes in their skins, then peel them (or not, as you choose), and cut them into cubes. Place them in an ovenproof bowl in the oven set to 250° F., to keep them very warm.

Cut up the onion and fry it with the bacon when you make the dressing; drain them both together. Omit the sugar from the dressing. Pour it over the potatoes, mix well, and serve at once.

Ham and Potato Salad

2 cups cubed cooked ham
2 cups cubed cooked potatoes
½ to 1 cup chopped celery with tops
4 hard-boiled eggs, finely chopped
Cottage Cheese Dressing (page 64)
Lettuce

Yield: 4 to 6 as a main dish

Here is a variation on classic potato salad. It goes very well on a picnic and will keep for several days in the refrigerator.

Combine the salad ingredients in a large bowl. Mix the dressing and pour it over, using the entire recipe. Chill for several hours to blend the flavors. Serve on beds of lettuce.

Curried Pear and Ham Salad

2 large pears, peeled and halved
Leafy salad greens
2 cups cooked rice
¾ cup diced cooked ham or turkey
⅓ cup raisins
¼ cup chopped salted peanuts
½ cup chopped celery
2 tablespoons chopped scallions
½ cup Mayonnaise II (page 20)
1 tablespoon lemon juice
1 teaspoon (or more) curry powder
Dash salt
Salad greens

Yield: 4 servings

This salad is wonderful for an elegant picnic supper. It travels well, but be sure to keep it cool. Try it with some homemade corn bread, young tender green beans, slightly salted, and a chilled crisp white wine.

Arrange the pears around the edge of a platter lined with greens (or use 4 individual salad bowls).

Combine the rice, ham or turkey, raisins, peanuts, celery, and scallions in a large bowl.

Mix together the mayonnaise, lemon juice, curry, and salt. Add more curry if that is to your taste. Pour over the salad and mix gently. Spoon onto the prepared greens and rearrange the pears around the edge, if necessary.

Polish Royal Salad

3 cups diced cooked potatoes
2 dill pickles, diced
2 cups diced cooked beets
¼ cup chopped scallions
3 cups diced tart apples, red-skinned and
    unpeeled
2 hard-boiled eggs, chopped
1 jar (5 ounces) herring fillets in oil or
    sour cream, drained
1 cup Mayonnaise I (page 19)
½ cup sour cream
1 tablespoon Dijon-style mustard
Lettuce

Yield: 8 servings as an appetizer
(4 to 6 as a main dish)

You can serve this colorful salad as an hors d'oeuvre or as a main dish for lunch or dinner. It also makes an unusual and interesting item on the buffet table.

Combine the vegetables with the apples, eggs, and herring. Mix the mayonnaise, sour cream, and mustard. Combine everything until well blended. Chill well. Serve on lettuce.

Variation

For a lower calorie version, substitute Mock Mayonnaise (page 62) for Mayonnaise I and plain yogurt for the sour cream.

Meat Salad

2 cups diced boiled potatoes
  (new potatoes, if possible)
1 cup chopped scallions
2 cups chopped celery, with some leaves
3 cups cubed lean cooked pot roast,
  boiled beef, or roast beef
3 large dill pickles, chopped
¼ cup capers (optional)
3 hard-boiled eggs, chopped
Creamy Mustard Dressing (page 22)
Salad greens
Cherry tomatoes or tomato slices

Yield: 6 servings

For some strange reason this salad—which is standard fare in both Germany and France—is not part of the American menu. Do try it as it is versatile, tasty, and a good way to use your leftover roast beef or pot roast. Serve it with a mixed green vegetable stir-fry and wedges of oatmeal soda bread or thick slices of dark rye or pumpernickel bread. And have a beer.

Combine the potatoes, scallions, celery, beef, pickles, capers, and eggs in a large bowl and mix well. Add the dressing (you will need at least 1 cup) and toss gently. Serve on a bed of salad greens and garnish with the tomatoes.

Beet Perfection Salad

2 cups diced cooked beets
1 cup shredded cabbage
1 envelope (¼ ounce) plain gelatin
1 tablespoon red wine vinegar
1 tablespoon lemon juice
2 tablespoons sugar
½ teaspoon salt
1 cup Creamy Yogurt Dressing (page 58)
Lettuce
Hard-boiled egg
Dill pickle

Yield: 6 to 8 servings

This molded salad has a marvelous color and is a good choice for a picnic or dish-to-pass supper.

If you use canned beets, drain off the liquid and reserve. If you cook the beets yourself—either by boiling in water to cover or in a pressure cooker—drain them and slip off the skins. Place the cooked beets in a bowl. Pour some boiling water over them, let it stand for several minutes, and then drain off the liquid, and reserve.

Combine the beets and cabbage in a bowl and set aside.

Add water to the beet liquid to make 1 cup. Soften the gelatin in the liquid, then add the vinegar, lemon juice, sugar, and salt. Heat gently in a saucepan, stirring, until the gelatin and sugar dissolve. Do *not* boil. Cool slightly, then stir in the dressing.

Pour this mixture over the vegetables, stir well, and place in a mold. Chill for at least 2 hours.

Unmold onto a bed of lettuce and garnish with hard-boiled egg wedges and slices of dill pickle.

Spinach Ring

2 envelopes (¼ ounce each) plain gelatin
2 teaspoons lemon juice
1 tablespoon white wine vinegar
2 teaspoons sugar
¾ cup boiling water
1 cup Mayonnaise II (page 20)
1 package (10 ounces) frozen chopped
   spinach or 1 bag (10 ounces) fresh
   spinach, steamed, drained, and
   chopped
½ cup finely chopped celery
1 small onion, finely chopped
¼ teaspoon onion salt
1 cup small-curd cottage cheese
Lettuce
Mayonnaise II or Creamy Mustard
   Dressing (page 22)

Yield: 8 to 10 servings
(6 as a main course)

In a large bowl, soften the gelatin in the lemon juice and vinegar and sprinkle the sugar over. Pour the boiling water over and whisk until the gelatin is dissolved. Place in the refrigerator until slightly thickened, about the consistency of egg white. Then beat in the mayonnaise.

While the gelatin mixture is cooling in the refrigerator, cook the spinach and drain it *very* well. Combine the spinach, celery, onion, onion salt, and cottage cheese. Stir this mixture into the gelatin-mayonnaise combination. Blend well. Pour into a 6-cup ring mold or a flat round bowl. Chill thoroughly. Unmold on lettuce. Pass additional mayonnaise or some Creamy Mustard Dressing.

Tuna Vegetable Mold

2 envelopes (¼ ounce each) plain gelatin
2 tablespoons red or white wine vinegar
1 cup hot water
1 cup Mayonnaise II (page 20)
1 can (6½ ounces) tuna, drained and
  flaked
¾ cup diced celery
¾ cup diced raw carrot
2 tablespoons minced onion
¼ cup diced sweet or dill pickle
1 hard-boiled egg, sliced
Salad greens
Mayonnaise

Yield: 4 to 6 servings

This molded salad makes an ideal main course on a hot summer evening. You can make it ahead of time and relax. Serve it with a combination of peas and rice, to which you have added some basil and Parmesan cheese, and some whole wheat rolls.

Soften the gelatin in the vinegar in a large bowl. Pour the boiling water over and whisk until the gelatin is dissolved. Stir in the mayonnaise and chill until slightly thickened.

Then fold in the tuna, celery, carrot, onion (you can use your processor to chop the vegetables), and pickle.

Arrange the sliced egg in the bottom of a 1½-quart mold, pour the mixture over, and chill until firm. Unmold on salad greens and serve with more mayonnaise.

Fresh Tomato Aspic

4 large tomatoes, halved and seeded
1 small onion, quartered
3 celery stalks, strings removed, in pieces
1 tablespoon sugar
1 teaspoon salt
1 bay leaf
2 envelopes (¼ ounce each) plain gelatin
½ cup cold water
3 tablespoons red or white wine vinegar
2 tablespoons lemon juice
½ teaspoon Worcestershire sauce
Salad greens
Guacamole (page 81)

Yield: 6 to 8 servings

Using the steel blade, finely chop the tomatoes, onion, and celery in a food processor. Simmer this mixture with the sugar, salt, and bay leaf for about 30 minutes, stirring occasionally.

Sprinkle the gelatin over the cold water in a large bowl. Pour the hot vegetable mixture over the gelatin and blend until the gelatin is dissolved. Add the vinegar, lemon juice, and Worcestershire. Stir well and remove the bay leaf.

Measure the mixture and add enough water to make 4 cups. Pour the aspic into a 4-cup mold. Chill for at least 2 hours.

Unmold the salad onto crisp salad greens and pour the Guacamole over the top. Serve at once.

7
Toppings

Any salad can be enhanced — in both taste and appearance — by some sort of topping. When you select a garnish, keep in mind the flavor, texture, and appearance of the salad. Quite simply you want something on top which tastes and looks good. So, as with most questions of good cooking, use common sense and a little imagination.

Following are some recipes for toppings that you can make yourself and suit a variety of tastes and situations. For something simple, consider the following:

Raw vegetables

Red or green peppers, in circles or thin strips
Celery, in strips, hearts, or stuffed with a savory cheese mix
Radishes, in slices or cut as roses
Carrots, grated or in matchstick strips
Tomatoes, sliced or in wedges, or cherry
Cucumbers, unpeeled, scored, sliced thin

Chives, minced
Parsley, chopped or in sprigs
Sprouts
Endive, in strips

Fruits

Avocado (brushed with lemon juice), in thin wedges
Olives, black or stuffed, whole or sliced
Strawberries in halves
Blueberries, raspberries
Cranberries, in whole sauce
Melon balls
Pineapple, in rings or chunks

Eggs and Cheese

Hard-boiled eggs, in slices or wedges
Hard-boiled egg yolk, sieved
Hard-boiled egg white, chopped
Firm cheeses, in cubes, strips, or shredded
Cottage cheese

Nuts, Seeds, Grains

Coconut, finely shredded or sliced
Nuts, raw or toasted, sliced, slivered, or
    chopped
Roasted soybeans, whole or chopped
Poppy seeds
Sesame seeds, raw or toasted
Sunflower seeds, raw, toasted, seasoned

Cereal Scrabble I

½ cup margarine or butter
1 tablespoon Worcestershire sauce
1 tablespoon soy sauce
1 tablespoon dried fines herbes
(1 teaspoon each parsley and chervil,
½ teaspoon each tarragon and chives,
or use a commercial mixture)
1 tablespoon dried parsley flakes
1 teaspoon garlic powder
½ teaspoon onion salt
1 cup dry-roasted peanuts
1 cup dry-roasted soy nuts
2 cups pretzel sticks
2 cups Cheerios® cereal
4 cups Wheat, Bran, and Corn Chex®
cereals

Yield: 10 cups

This recipe has been part of my life since I was a child. If you don't sprinkle it on a salad, serve it as a cocktail snack.

Set the oven at 275° F. In a large roasting pan, melt the margarine in the oven. Add the seasonings and mix well. Then add the remaining ingredients and stir well to blend.

Bake until brown and crunchy, stirring occasionally. This takes about 1 hour, depending on how often you open the oven door and stir. Cool and store in an airtight container.

Cereal Scrabble II

¼ cup margarine
¼ teaspoon garlic powder
¼ teaspoon onion salt
2 teaspoons lemon juice
4 teaspoons Worcestershire sauce
7 cups cereal (Kellogg's Crispix® is best, but you can also use a combination of Chex® and Cheerios®)
1 cup mixed nuts
1 cup pretzels in rings

Yield: 9 cups

Here is a somewhat simpler recipe than the preceding, milder in flavor, quicker to make.

Melt the margarine in a roasting pan in the oven set at 250° F. Remove from the oven and stir in the seasonings. Add the cereal, nuts, and pretzels. Mix until the cereal is coated.

Bake for about 45 minutes or until brown and crunchy, stirring occasionally. Cool and store in an airtight container.

Cheese Sprinkle

1 cup grated Parmesan, Romano, Swiss,
   cheddar, or hard Gouda
2 teaspoons celery, poppy, or sesame
   seeds
2 teaspoons dried parsley flakes
½ teaspoon dried oregano or marjoram
½ teaspoon dried basil
¼ teaspoon dried thyme
Salt and pepper

Yield: About 1 cup

You can vary the herbs and seeds to your taste. If you make this with any of the dry Italian cheeses, it will keep for ages in the refrigerator.

Mix everything together in a jar or a bowl, adding salt and pepper to taste, and shake or stir well. Store in an airtight container in the refrigerator.

Crunchy Topping

2 cups rolled oats
⅓ cup wheat germ
⅓ cup grated Parmesan cheese
¼ teaspoon seasoned salt (optional)
1 teaspoon dried oregano
½ teaspoon dried thyme
¼ cup margarine or butter, melted

Yield: 3 cups

I keep a jar of this topping in my refrigerator at all times. It is wonderful on mixed green salads or on cooked vegetables. It also goes very well on soups, hot or cold.

Preheat the oven to 350° F.

Combine the dry ingredients in a large baking pan and mix well. Pour the melted margarine or butter over, stir to coat everything, and bake for 15 to 20 minutes, or until light golden brown. Cool and store, tightly covered, in the refrigerator.

Fruit and Nut Topping

½ cup raisins
¼ cup diced dried pineapple
¼ cup diced dried apricots
¼ cup chopped dried apples
¼ cup diced dried papaya (if you can get it)
¼ cup shredded coconut
¼ cup sunflower seeds
¼ cup sesame seeds
¼ cup pumpkin seeds
¼ cup dry-roasted peanuts
¼ cup soy nuts
¼ cup raw cashews

Yield: About 3 cups

This goes very well over any mixed fruit salad. If you sprinkle it on a molded salad, it adds a lovely color and texture. There are people who serve this mixture with cocktails and there are people in my house who snack on it. So hide it for your salads!

Put all the ingredients in a large jar with a screw lid. Shake vigorously to mix everything. Store tightly covered.

Granola

¼ cup honey
¼ cup sunflower oil
1 teaspoon vanilla extract
½ teaspoon salt
2 cups rolled wheat
2 cups rolled oats
½ cup sesame seeds
½ cup sunflower seeds
½ cup chopped walnuts
½ cup shredded coconut

Yield: 6 cups

There are many recipes for granola, but this one makes an ideal topping for mixed fruit salads. If you can't find the rolled wheat, substitute 3 cups rolled oats and 1 cup raw wheat germ.

Heat the honey and oil in a small saucepan until warm and blended. Stir in the vanilla and salt. Mix the remaining ingredients, except the coconut, in a large baking pan. Pour the honey-oil mixture over and stir to coat everything well.

Bake at 350° F. for about 30 minutes, stirring every 5 minutes. Do watch it, as it can burn easily. When the granola is nearly done, sprinkle the coconut over the top and continue baking until it is browned (this takes only a few minutes). Store in an airtight container in a cool, dry place.

Marinated Tofu

1 block (½ pound) tofu
1 teaspoon dried oregano
1 large garlic clove, pressed
¼ cup olive oil
¼ cup red wine vinegar
¼ cup red wine
¼ cup soy sauce
Freshly ground black pepper

Yield: About 1½ cups

Little cubes of savory tofu add zest and protein to mixed greens and to raw and cooked vegetable salads.

Drain and press the tofu to remove excess water. Cut it into small cubes.

Toast the oregano in a small frying pan over medium heat until it becomes aromatic. Be careful not to burn it.

Combine the garlic, oil, vinegar, wine, soy sauce, and pepper to taste in a saucepan. Add the oregano. Bring the mixture to a boil and simmer for a few minutes.

Put the tofu cubes in a large bowl and pour the hot marinade over. Marinate overnight in the refrigerator. This mixture can be marinated for several days, and you can dip out the cubes as you need them.

Seasoned Croutons

3 cups firm whole wheat or white bread
 cubes
2 tablespoons butter
Garlic powder or pressed garlic (optional)
½ teaspoon salt
1 teaspoon paprika
About ¼ cup grated Parmesan cheese
Minced chives, oregano, thyme, or dill
Poppy seeds (optional)

Yield: 3 cups

Croutons can be made two ways. One is to butter the bread, sprinkle with garlic powder, if desired, cut it into cubes, and bake the cubes in a 350° F. oven until toasted, about 15 minutes. The far more common rule, however, is to cut the bread in cubes and fry them in some butter—to which you can add garlic—until they are crusty and brown.

Then drop the croutons into a paper bag to which you have added the seasonings. Close the bag and shake it until the croutons are evenly coated. Cool and store in an airtight container.

Savory Nuts

2 cups chopped or sliced nuts
2 tablespoons melted butter or oil
Celery salt, garlic salt, onion salt,
  cayenne pepper, or paprika (or a
  combination)

Yield: 2 cups

Chopped seasoned nuts add crunch and a delightful flavor to any salad, providing the seasoning fits. Use almonds, walnuts, pecans, peanuts, or cashews, or a combination. Almonds can be sliced or slivered instead of chopped.

Place the nuts and butter or oil in a large skillet and cook slowly, shaking the pan and stirring the nuts, until they are light brown. While they are hot, sprinkle them generously with seasonings. Drain on brown paper.

Instead of toasting them in a frying pan, the nuts can be baked at 300° F. for about 20 minutes. Stir occasionally.

Cool the nuts and store tightly covered in the refrigerator.

Variation

Seasoned Soy Nuts. Substitute soy sauce for the butter or oil and omit the salt. Season with paprika.

Spiced Nuts

⅓ cup sugar
¼ cup cornstarch
Dash salt
1½ teaspoons cinnamon
½ teaspoon allspice
¼ teaspoon nutmeg
¼ teaspoon ginger
1 egg white
2 tablespoons cold water
1 cup nut meats (pecans or walnuts)

Yield: 1 cup

Here is an unusual topping for fruit salads or for greens combined with fruits.

Sift the dry ingredients into a shallow pan. Combine the egg white and water and beat slightly. Dip the nuts into the egg white mixture and drop them one at a time into the mixed dry ingredients. Roll them around lightly.

Place the nuts on a baking sheet and bake at 250° F. for about 1½ hours. Take them from the oven and shake off the excess sugar. When the nuts are cool and crisp, store them in an airtight container in the refrigerator.

Index